Yes! Cats Win!

by Vincent York
illustrated by Delfina Bryant

Practice Decodable 13

McGraw Hill Education

Bothell, WA • Chicago, IL • Columbus, OH • New York, NY

MHEonline.com

Send all inquiries to:
McGraw-Hill Education
8787 Orion Place
Columbus, OH 43240

ISBN: 978-0-02-144965-1
MHID: 0-02-144965-1

Printed in China.

9 10 11 12 13 DSS 27 26 25 24 23

Vans were in lots.

Fans were in stands.

Vic sprints.
Run, Vic!
Val yelps.

Vic trips.
Did Vic quit?
Not yet!

Did the Cats win?

Yes!

It was fun for kids!

It was fun for fans!